Robyn Gool

W
WHITAKER
HOUSE

Unless otherwise indicated, all Scripture quotations are taken from the *King James Version* (KJV) of the Holy Bible.

Scripture quotations marked (AMP) are taken from *The Amplified Bible,* Old Testament © 1965, 1987 by the Zondervan Corporation. The Amplified New Testament © 1958, 1987 by The Lockman Foundation. Used by permission.

Scripture quotations marked (NIV) are from the Holy Bible, *New International Version,* © 1973, 1978, 1984 by the International Bible Society. Used by permission.

FOR SINGLES ONLY

Robyn Gool
More than Conquerors Ministries
P.O. Box 240433
Charlotte, NC 28224

ISBN: 0-88368-648-1
Printed in the United States of America
Copyright © 1987 by Robyn Gool

Whitaker House
30 Hunt Valley Circle
New Kensington, PA 15068

Library of Congress Cataloging-in-Publication Data

Gool, Robyn, 1953–
  For singles only / by Robyn Gool.
     p. cm.
  ISBN 0-88368-648-1 (pbk. alk. paper)
  1. Single people—Religious life. I. Title.
  BV4596.S5 G66 1987
  248.8'4—dc21   00-012688

1 2 3 4 5 6 7 8 9 10 11 12 13 / 09 08 07 06 05 04 03 02 01

Contents

Introduction

Have you ever heard the story about the three Frenchmen who were visiting the United States for the first time? Upon their arrival they decided to take a stroll along the beach to enjoy the scenery. Since they knew no English, they thought this would be a good way to begin to acquaint themselves with American life.

As they were walking along, they noticed that everyone seemed to be hurrying past them. Curious, they followed the crowd, which stopped in front of a concession stand. The man behind the counter was shouting, "Hot dogs, hot dogs. Who wants hot dogs? Twenty-five cents!"

"I, I, I," cried the hungry crowd. So the first Frenchman picked up the word *I*.

The second Frenchman, being intrigued by the sales pitch, picked up the expression *twenty-five cents.*

As the crowd rushed together to form a line for their refreshments, the third Frenchman noticed a man pushing and shouting, "I'm first in line! I'm first in line!" So he picked up that phrase.

After leaving the beach en route to their hotel, the trio of foreigners happened to pass an alley where they noticed a man lying on the pavement in a pool of blood. Upon examination, they saw that he had been badly beaten and stabbed. Checking his pulse, they learned that the man was dead. As they stood there pondering what to do, suddenly a police car drew up and an officer of the law got out.

Rushing to the side of the fallen man, the officer looked up at the three French visitors and asked, "Who did this?"

Not understanding a word of the inquiry, the three Europeans just stared at the policeman with a puzzled look on their faces.

"I asked you who did this!" repeated the officer brusquely.

Recognizing the tone of authority in his voice, the first Frenchman decided he'd better use the only English word he knew. "I," he replied with a smile.

"What did you do it for?" demanded the policeman, his anger rising.

"Twenty-five cents," offered the second Frenchman, eager to join the conversation.

"Why you cold-blooded cutthroats," exploded the policeman. "You're all three going to get the electric chair for this!"

At that, the third Frenchman chimed in enthusiastically, "I'm first in line!"

Do you know what got these fellows into trouble? A lack of knowledge. Today, many singles, young and old, are having difficulty in their personal relationships for that same reason. Ignorance has caused countless numbers of unmarried people to experience trouble, hurt, and abuse. Some have been so badly scarred on the inside they may never recover.

What is the answer? The Word of God. In Proverbs 11:9, Solomon tells us, *Through knowledge shall the just be delivered.* The purpose of this book is to provide insight to singles from the Word of God about dating, marriage, and sex so that total success and victory in these areas can be enjoyed. I urge you to open your mind and heart to the message contained in these pages. As you read, ask the Holy Spirit to lead you into the truth so that you will be delivered through the knowledge that comes only from God.

1

Jesus Is the Answer

1

Jesus Is the Answer

One of the strongest deceptions used by the Enemy of God is the idea that marriage is the solution to loneliness. This suggestion is especially effective with single people because it seems so plausible. Unfortunately, as logical and appealing as it may seem, it just isn't so. The answer to loneliness is not just human companionship, as good as that may be. Like all problems of human existence, the basic solution is found only in the Word of God.

In Matthew 6:33 the Lord gave us the key to happy and successful living when He told His disciples, *"But seek ye first the kingdom of God, and his righteousness; and all these things* [that you need] *shall be added unto you."* The solution to any problem you may face in life is found only in Jesus Christ and in seeking first the things of God.

So many young people seem to feel that if they could only get married, then all of their problems would be solved. You may feel that way yourself. Unfortunately, it just isn't true. Marriage is not the answer to your problems. The solution to any problem of life must come through the Word of God, not just by a change of circumstances or situation. If you can't handle your personal life on your own, you won't be any more successful with a mate.

The Enemy will approach you and whisper in your ear that the answer to your problems is to get married. Don't listen to him. Marriage was not instituted by God as a "quick fix" for personal problems. Anyone who thinks that way is deceived. Marriage is a wonderful institution, one from which most people will benefit in many ways. But it must not be entered into as a "way out" of troubles. To do so is not to avoid trouble; it is to *guarantee* it!

Marriage was not instituted as a solution to loneliness. A person must be able to handle loneliness whether he's single or married. Even the happiest of married people experience occasional feelings of loneliness. That's just part of being human. The answer is not constant human companionship as much as it is continual fellow-ship with God. The only true solution to human loneliness is a closer walk with the Creator.

Three Steps to Happiness

Delight thyself also in the LORD; *and he shall give thee the desires of thine heart. Commit thy way unto the* LORD; *trust also in him; and he shall bring it to pass....Rest in the* LORD, *and wait patiently for him.*   (Psalm 37:4–5, 7)

In this passage the psalmist provides us with sound counsel for successful living. Notice especially verse four: *"Delight thyself also in the* LORD; *and he shall give thee the desires of thine heart."* I dare say that most people desire to be married at one time or another in their lives. That may be the desire of your heart right now. If so, notice how you receive the desires of your heart: by delighting yourself in God. The Bible declares that if you will delight yourself in God, He will give you the very things you desire most in life.

Verse five says that if you will commit your way (your life) unto the Lord, He will bring *"it"* to pass. Bring *what* to pass? The desires of your heart.

Finally, verse seven says to rest in God. Once a matter has been entrusted to God, then wait patiently upon Him, allowing Him time to work things out for the best.

So here then are the three steps to finding the right mate, the perfect life partner: (1) Delight yourself in God, (2) commit your way to Him, and (3) wait upon Him in trust and patience, allowing Him to do the work for you.

Once you have committed your way to the Lord, be at rest. If you're not at rest, then you're operating in unbelief. If you're anxious, fretful, or worried; if you're in despair; if you're frustrated; or if you're impatient, then you must not expect anything from God because you are not operating in faith. (See James 1:5–8.)

It is not enough just to pray, to ask God to do something. Our Lord said that when we pray, we must *believe* that we receive (Mark 11:24). You cannot worry and believe at the same time.

Nor is it enough to "confess" that you have the thing you have asked of God in prayer. Confession is fine, but it alone will not produce results. It doesn't matter how many times you speak the Word of God, how many times you pray, fast, sing, or confess victory; without real faith the desire will not be forthcoming. Faith commits to God; then it *rests*. Once you have committed your way to the Lord, wait upon Him in patience, confident that He will perform what He has promised.

Remember, the solution to your problems in life is not a husband or a wife; *it is God.* Whatever the situation you may be facing in your life at this moment, attack it with the Word of God. Don't depend on marriage or any other human institution or agency for your solution. Don't even depend upon your own knowledge or wisdom or ability. Instead, take that problem to the Lord in prayer. Seek first the Lord and His righteousness. Commit your way to Him. Ask Him for His solution. Then rest in peace, secure in the knowledge that He will provide the perfect answer in His time.

2

Prepare Yourself

2

Prepare Yourself

D o you have high standards in your selection of a mate? If so, that's good. You should have high standards. You should want your future mate to be the best in the world.

But remember, he or she will also have high standards.

That means that in order to be worthy of that kind of ideal mate, you must begin now to prepare yourself to be a good reward for that great person you expect to marry one day.

There are so many young people, Christian and non-Christian alike, who go through life boasting of what a perfect mate they are going to have someday—how good-looking, well-groomed, and well-mannered their future "dreamboat" will be. That's all well and good. But too many times the person doing the talking is just the opposite; he or she is overweight or out of shape, slovenly in appearance, and self-centered. How can this person possibly expect to attract a top-notch, cream-of-the-crop person? If his ideal has all those positive traits, why would that ideal person ever want someone who is lacking in those areas?

It's not enough to have high ideals and standards in your choice of a mate; you must also have something to offer in return.

Remember, if you want the best, prepare yourself to *be* the best.

Preparation includes many things. It means getting yourself in shape physically, mentally, emotionally, financially, socially, and, above all, spiritually.

If you want to attract a good mate, get in shape physically. After all, not many people want a "heavyweight" lover!

As important as it is, physical appearance is not everything. To be truly attractive requires discipline in every area of life. God commanded us to love Him with all our hearts, souls, minds, and strength (Mark 12:30). He didn't leave anything out. That means we have an obligation to develop the whole person—spirit, soul, and body.

Spiritual Preparation

If ye then be risen with Christ, seek those things which are above.   (Colossians 3:1)

*But seek ye **first** the kingdom of God, and his righteousness; and all these things shall be added unto you.*
                    (Matthew 6:33, emphasis added)

As Christians, our first duty is to prepare ourselves spiritually. Jesus said that we are to seek *first* the kingdom of God and His righteousness in our lives. That means that we should get to know our heavenly Father. The only way to get to know a person is to spend time in his presence. We do that with God by reading the Bible, praying, meditating on His Word, and worshipping and fellowshipping with other believers on a regular basis. The more time we spend with the Lord, the more we become like Him and understand Him and His ways and Word.

Have you ever been around people who recoil the instant you mention anything spiritual? The moment the conversation turns to the Lord, many people become uncomfortable. They can talk sports or politics or even the weather for hours on end, but for some reason the slightest mention of God makes them nervous. That's because they really don't know anything about Him. Such people have undeveloped spirits.

That can happen even to Christians. A person can be a believer and yet never spend any time developing his spirit-man. He can be an intellectual giant with a tremendous physique, yet still be a spiritual midget. To some extent, that was my problem at one point in my life.

When I met Marilyn, the young woman who was later to become my wife, I was a student at Oral Roberts University in Tulsa, Oklahoma. I had gone there on a tennis scholarship. I lived and breathed tennis. That's all I talked about because that was all I thought about. I now know that whatever a person talks about most reveals what he thinks about most, because *"out of the abundance of the heart the mouth speaketh"* (Matthew 12:34).

As a result of my overemphasis on sports, I had neglected my spiritual development for years. Although I had been born again at age nine, by the time I entered college I was a spiritual weakling. It didn't take me long to realize that Marilyn was far more spiritually developed than I was.

Realizing that both partners in a relationship should be mature spiritually as well as mentally and emotionally, Marilyn's spirituality motivated me to study the Bible. I knew that she was just what I had been searching for in a woman all my life, so I wanted to come up to her level of spiritual maturity.

I studied and studied to prepare myself for our future life together. I knew that as the man of the house, it would be my responsibility to act as the head of the home, and that I would set the spiritual tone for the family. So I applied myself to the Word of God to prepare myself for spiritual leadership.

The fall semester of my sophomore year, I was called into the ministry. I decided to stay out of school the next semester and minister at home in Detroit, Michigan. There I had the opportunity to share the Word of God with the young people of my church. We would go out witnessing to others and had some wonderful experiences in the Lord.

When I returned to school the next semester, I met Marilyn again. This time it was different. All I could talk about was Jesus. Marilyn knew right away that something had happened to me. She realized that I had grown a great deal spiritually. She was more interested in me than ever because she recognized that I had so applied myself to the Word that I had surpassed even her level of spiritual development. She had always said that she would never marry a man who was not serving the Lord, and that the man she married would have to be willing to fulfill the role of the spiritual head of her home. She knew then that "that man" was me.

All this took place because I devoted the time and effort necessary to prepare myself for marriage by developing myself spiritually, as well as mentally and physically.

Mental Preparation

And be not conformed to this world: but be ye transformed by the renewing of your mind, that ye may prove what is that good, and acceptable, and perfect, will of God. (Romans 12:2)

To prepare yourself mentally, start by renewing your mind through the Word of God. Get it so full of God's Word that you talk in line with it and not in line with the world. Study the Bible. Pray and commune with the Lord until you think like Jesus.

In the Old Testament, God spoke to Joshua and told him,

This book of the law shall not depart out of thy mouth; but thou shalt meditate therein day and night, that thou mayest observe to do according to all that is written therein: for then thou shalt

*make thy way prosperous, and then thou shalt
have good success.*   (Joshua 1:8)

Later on, Solomon wrote these words of
wisdom:

*My son, attend to my words; incline thine ear
unto my sayings. Let them not depart from
thine eyes; keep them in the midst of thine heart.
For they are life unto those that find them, and
health to all their flesh.*   (Proverbs 4:20–22)

To gain mental maturity, the first step is to
spend time daily reading, studying, and meditating on the Word of God. It will be health and
life to you. It will renew and refresh your mind.

But knowledge of the Bible is not enough.
There must also be an accompanying commitment to knowledge of every aspect of daily
living.

The Christian ought to be the best in whatever he does, because he applies himself. Solomon told us, *"Whatsoever thy hand findeth to do,
do it with* [all] *thy might"* (Ecclesiastes 9:10). That
includes schoolwork as well as Bible study.

When God said through the prophet Hosea,
"My people are destroyed for lack of knowledge"
(Hosea 4:6), He was specifically referring to
knowledge of Himself (verse 1). However,
this principle can apply to everything in life.

Therefore, intellectual knowledge—the knowledge gained in school and college—is very important, as well.

In the New Testament, the apostle Paul wrote at least six times that he would not have us to be ignorant. (See Romans 1:13; 11:25; 1 Corinthians 10:1; 12:1; 2 Corinthians 1:8; 1 Thessalonians 4:13.) Jesus told His disciples that to succeed in this life, they would have to be as wise as serpents (Matthew 10:16). Later He pointed out, *"The children of this world are in their generation wiser than the children of light"* (Luke 16:8), implying that this should not be so. What the Lord was telling us in these verses is that we must develop our mental as well as our spiritual capacities.

Physical Preparation

For ye are bought with a price: therefore glorify God in your body, and in your spirit, which are God's. (1 Corinthians 6:20)

Although marriage is instituted by God, it is not merely a spiritual union. Marriage is not made up of just churchgoing and Bible reading. Jesus said that when a man and woman are married, they become *"one flesh"* (Matthew 19:6). Therefore, the flesh—the physical body—is as important in marriage as the mind or the spirit.

In order to fully prepare yourself for marriage, you need to get your body into shape. Whether you are a man or a woman, your future partner wants (and deserves!) a physically attractive mate. After all, nobody wants to be married to a slob! That doesn't mean that we all have to be athletic superstars; it just means that we all need to be the best we can possibly be—for our Lord and ourselves, as well as for our spouses.

Physical training is not easy. Like everything worthwhile, it requires discipline and self-denial. You may have to go on a diet or lift weights or take up jogging or bicycle riding. Whatever it takes, make up your mind that you are going to get into good physical condition—and stay that way!

Get a mental picture of the way you want to look. Hold on to that image. Don't let anything keep you from your daily exercise program.

Remember, you are someone's ideal mate. You are someone's answer to prayer. Keep that in mind as you wait for the Lord to reveal to you your ideal, His perfect answer for you.

Prepare yourself physically! Bring that body under subjection. If you're overweight, take authority over your body and bring it into line with God's Word. If necessary, put a muzzle on your jaws! You can do it. All it takes is will power.

There is no magic formula for weight loss. It is a simple scientific principle. To lose weight, you simply have to burn more calories than you take in. That means increasing exercise and decreasing eating. There is no other way!

This is not a quick fix. It is a way of life. Once begun, it must be kept up—from now on. Otherwise, once you reach your goal, you will go back to your old habits and soon gain back everything you have lost and more!

Change your eating habits! That's the only way to take off weight and keep it off. Instead of stuffing your face with high-calorie foods and snacks, take up walking. Fight your craving for food by walking it off. You'll lose not only the craving, but also the excess pounds.

Some people do have trouble losing weight because of glandular problems. You may be one of them. But even if you are, there is something you can do. Take your problem to the Lord in prayer. Claim your healing in the name of Jesus. On the authority of Mark 11:23–24, speak to your mountain—your glandular condition—and order it to be *"cast into the sea"* (verse 23). Then hold firm to your profession of faith that by the stripes of Jesus you are healed (1 Peter 2:24).

You can gain the victory over your physical body. The apostle Paul said, *"But I keep under my body, and bring it into subjection"* (1 Corinthians 9:27). Keeping under the body and bringing it into subjection implies giving it proper nourishment, rest, and exercise. If Paul could do that by the power of the Lord, then so can you. You can get into shape physically. As you do, you will be preparing yourself to be that ideal mate you want to have one day.

Financial Preparation

"For wisdom is a defence, and money is a defence" (Ecclesiastes 7:12).

In this verse, as throughout the book of Proverbs, wise Solomon counsels us not only to be wise, but also to pay attention to our finances. *"Be thou diligent to know the state of thy flocks, and look well to thy herds"* (Proverbs 27:23). In other words, if we are to be successful in this life, we must learn to "take care of business."

This is especially true for young people who are preparing to launch forth into marriage and life outside of their parents' home. You cannot afford to wait until you are married to begin to prepare financially. You must begin now.

If you are still a student, you may not feel that you are able yet to start preparing financially. But you can. No matter how young you

how to cook for her family. If you are a young woman and you don't yet know how to cook, it's time you began to learn. Ask your mother, grandmother, or a friend to help you learn. If you have no one to teach you, take a course in home economics while in high school, college, or technical school. If none of these avenues is available, buy a good cookbook and start to learn on your own. The Lord will help you if you really want to learn. It will be well worth your while later on when you have a husband and a family.

Verse twenty in *The Amplified Bible* says, *"She opens her hand to the poor; yes, she reaches out her filled hands to the needy [whether in body, mind or spirit]."* A virtuous woman, a woman of God, is one who can meet the needs of other people. She may not always have the finances herself to meet the need, but she has the mind of Christ. She spends time with the Lord and allows Him to show her how to be creative in order to meet the needs of people around her.

That is good wisdom for both men and women of God, particularly those who are preparing for marriage and other aspects of adult life. Learn how to develop your inborn talents and abilities. Exercise the gifts that God has given to you in preparation for that man or woman you are seeking as a life partner.

Be concerned about others. Have compassion. Share what you have with those in need. The Lord has promised that it will come back to you in multiplied abundance (Luke 6:38). Learn to give. That's the first and best step toward financial maturity!

Preparation for Young Ladies

"She openeth her mouth with wisdom; and in her tongue is the law of kindness" (Proverbs 31:26).

This verse calls to mind what the apostle Paul had to say in Colossians 4:6: *"Let your speech be alway with grace, seasoned with salt, that ye may know how ye ought to answer every man."* As a young woman preparing for marriage and adult life, you need to be learning to allow God to mold your conversation so that it always exhorts, comforts, and edifies. God opposes murmuring, complaining, and scoffing. When you open your mouth, speak wisdom—not foolishness and disdain. Don't be one who causes strife or disharmony. Be part of the solution, not part of the problem—especially in the home.

In Proverbs 21:19 Solomon said, *"It is better to dwell in the wilderness, than with a contentious and an angry woman."* Solomon said that it would be better for a man to live in the desert than with an angry, argumentative woman. Since he had seven hundred wives and three hundred concubines, he ought to have known what he was talking about!

In Proverbs 27:15 he wrote, *"A continual dropping in a very rainy day and a contentious woman are alike."* Notice Solomon's estimation of a nagging wife: "A complaining woman is like a dripping faucet—both will drive you crazy!" That should be a lesson to all women, but especially to you as a future wife and mother. Just as a leaky faucet can rob a person of sleep, so continual griping and nagging can rob a home of peace and tranquillity.

The apostle Peter spoke of husbands being won without a word by the conversation of their wives (1 Peter 3:1). He urged women not to depend upon outward adornment for their beauty, but on the *"ornament of a meek and quiet spirit, which is in the sight of God of great price"* (verse 4).

Don't be a *"contentious woman"* (Proverbs 27:15). Starting right now, learn to be disciplined in your conversation. Work to develop *"a meek and quiet spirit"* (1 Peter 3:4). Be gentle. Be kind. Be loving. Understand that faith works by love (Galatians 5:6). You can pray and ask God for the desires of your heart; you can confess that you have received your request, but unless you are walking in love toward others (especially your mate), your faith will not operate for you. Without love, faith will not produce.

In speaking of the virtuous woman (or the effective homemaker), Solomon said, *"She looks well to how things go in her household, and the bread of idleness [gossip, discontent and self-pity] she will not eat"* (Proverbs 31:27 AMP). In order to prepare for a successful marriage, you must learn not to be lazy or to waste time in idleness, gossip, and feeling sorry for yourself. Instead, learn how to organize your day. Make use of every moment God has given to you.

There is no reason for anyone to ever complain that there are not enough hours in the day to get everything accomplished. We Christians have the Greater One within us. He will help us to get things done faster and more effectively than an unbeliever could ever do them.

Learn to budget your moments as well as your money. Dedicate your time to God's glory. Use it to honor Him, and He will multiply it as He did the loaves and fishes. (See Matthew 14:15–21.)

Benjamin Franklin once said, "Dost thou love life? Then do not squander time, for that is the stuff life is made of." Time is a precious gift from our heavenly Father. Don't waste it on things like soap operas. You are much too valuable to God, your family, and yourself to squander the best moments of your life by watching trash. Use the time you would have spent watching daytime television by investing it in self-improvement. Sign up for a course in aerobics or rhythmic dance. Learn to speak a foreign language or to restore antique furniture or to do embroidery or macramé. Do volunteer work at a local nursing home, children's hospital, or home for the mentally handicapped. If nothing else, find a part-time job and bring in some extra income. The list is endless; so are the rewards.

Remember, time is the one gift from God you cannot replace or recall. You can only *redeem* it (Ephesians 5:16).

If you want to have a happy marriage and home, learn to discipline your tongue and use your time wisely.

Preparation for Young Men

But thou, O man of God, flee these things; and follow after righteousness, godliness, faith, love, patience, meekness. Fight the good fight of faith, lay hold on eternal life, whereunto thou art also called, and hast professed a good profession before many witnesses.

(1 Timothy 6:11–12)

Believe it or not, one of these days you'll want to give up the life of a carefree bachelor. You'll want to get married and settle down, put down roots, and raise a family of your own. Sooner or later it happens to just about every young man. That's because God has placed that desire deep within the heart of men. Sometimes it just takes a little while for that desire to rise to the surface.

In the meantime, you may well have the urge to get out and "sow some wild oats" before it's too late. If so, that's understandable. That's the way our society thinks. For generations we have heard that boys will be boys, that they just have to get it out of their systems one way or another. It's understandable that you may feel that way. But it's not scriptural.

Read what the great apostle Paul wrote to his "spiritual son," Timothy. You will notice that he made no mention of the fact that Timothy needed to sow some wild oats now and then. Paul didn't seem to think that young Timothy needed to "get his run out" (as some people say). Instead, he called him a *"man of God"* (1 Timothy 6:11). He counseled him to flee youthful lusts and to follow after *"righteousness, godliness, faith, love, patience, meekness"* (verse 11).

In chapter four, Paul wrote to Timothy, *"Let no man despise thy youth; but be thou an example* *of the believers, in word, in conversation, in charity, in spirit, in faith, **in purity**"* (verse 12, emphasis added). Then later on, in 2 Timothy 2:1, he exhorted his young disciple, *"Thou therefore, my son, be strong in the grace that is in Christ Jesus."*

This is God's counsel to you as a Christian young man. He wants you to remember who you are in Christ Jesus and to act like it! Part of the proper behavior of a Christian young man is respect for women.

In 1 Timothy 5:2, Paul advised Timothy to treat *"the elder women as mothers; the younger as sisters, **with all purity**"* (emphasis added). There's that expression again—*"with all purity."* That is the key.

Part of the instruction that Paul gave to Timothy was, *"Fight the good fight of faith"* (1 Timothy 6:12). The fight of faith is in the mind. The Bible speaks of *"casting down imaginations, and every high thing that exalteth itself against the knowledge of God, and bringing into captivity every thought to the obedience of Christ"* (2 Corinthians 10:5). Nowhere is this needed more than when in the company of a lovely young lady. In that situation, if your thoughts are not consistent with the Word of God, then throw out those thoughts. Reprogram yourself. Concentrate on things that are true, honest, just, pure, lovely, and of good report (Philippians 4:8).

Remember, treat older women like your mother, younger women like your sister, and do so *in all purity.*

Women—both young and old—like to be treated like queens. Begin now to prepare yourself to do just that. Learn some etiquette! Learn to open doors for women. Remove your hat or cap in the presence of a lady. Stand when she is introduced to you or when she leaves the table.

And this doesn't apply just to older women. It applies to your date, as well. It also applies to your wife when you have one. Learn to help her with her coat. Hold her chair when she sits down. Compliment her on her appearance. Show your lady that that is exactly what she is to you—a lady. By your actions and speech, show her that she means something to you, that she is valuable and precious to you. That's good etiquette. That's godliness. Besides all that, it works! She'll love it!

Young man, be a gentleman. You'll never regret it, and she'll never forget it!

3

The Godly Woman's Approach to Relationships

3

The Godly Woman's Approach to Relationships

Wait on the Lord

For the husband is the head of the wife, even as Christ is the head of the church.
—Ephesians 5:23

God has planned the home in such a way that there is unity of command. Although both husband and wife share the responsibility of establishing and maintaining the family relationship, it is God's will that the husband fill the role of the head of the house. He is to be the spiritual leader, the "high priest" of the family. It is his duty and responsibility to set the spiritual tone for the home.

Since God has set the husband as head of the family unit, it is logical that it is the man who is to take the lead in establishing the marriage relationship. By that I mean it is to be the man, not the woman, who is to be the initiator of the relationship.

In Proverbs 18:22 we read these words: *"Whoso findeth a wife findeth a good thing, and obtaineth favour of the LORD."* You will notice that the Bible doesn't say that whoever finds a husband finds favor with the Lord; rather, it is whoever finds a wife finds a good thing. This is evidence that, in God's eyes, it is the man who is to be the seeker, not the woman.

Now, that is not discrimination on the part of man or God. It is simply God's plan and His will that the one who will ultimately be responsible for leading and providing for the family be the one who takes the major role in creating that family relationship.

Many young people today, both Christian and non-Christian alike, don't seem to understand this truth. Some young ladies seem to think it is their privilege and right in this "liberated age" to chase after young men. Either they flaunt themselves brazenly before them or they use their feminine charms to entice them into a relationship. Either way, it's the young woman, not the young man, who is initiating the romance. According to the Scriptures, that is not God's way of bringing a couple together.

One danger of that kind of activity is that once it's begun—once a young lady starts to take the lead—she has to keep it up the rest of her life. The fellow gets so accustomed to being led around like a puppy, he loses his manly initiative. Many times a young lady will chase after a young man until she catches him, only to find out that once she's got him, she doesn't want him anymore. Part of the reason for this loss of interest is that, whether she realizes it or not, she has lost respect for him because she knows she can manipulate him. Even if the relationship lasts, it's not a good foundation for marriage. A marriage in which the woman is the aggressor is not built on the firm foundation of God's eternal plan.

If you are a young lady, don't chase a man! Let him chase you! Don't go looking for a boyfriend or a husband; let God's choice come searching for you. If you're the right one for him, he'll find you. He has help—the Lord is looking out for him and for you!

Let the man do the chasing. That's God's way, His plan. But it's not only good theology, it's also good psychology—it works! Try it; you'll like it!

Know Who You Are in Christ

For he [God] *hath made him* [Christ] *to be sin for us, who knew no sin; that we might be made the righteousness of God in him.*

(2 Corinthians 5:21)

Young lady, you should know who you are in Christ. If you do, you will maintain your proper role and position in your everyday life. This is especially important in dating. You must remember that you're not a sex symbol. You are the righteousness of God in Christ Jesus.

> *Neither yield ye your members* [your body] *as instruments of unrighteousness unto sin: but yield yourselves unto God, as those that are alive from the dead, and your members* [your body] *as instruments of righteousness unto God.* (Romans 6:13)

As the righteousness of God, your body is sacred. It's holy ground. You're not a "playmate" or a toy. You are the living embodiment of Jesus Christ Himself!

Sometimes it may be necessary to force that image onto a man. He may not recognize or appreciate who you are as a Christian. He may try to make you over into the image he has for you. He may attempt to make you his plaything. You don't have to stand for that. If he doesn't recognize who you are, tell him! Let him know that you are a lady and that you expect to treated as such!

As a lady, you ought to have a high opinion of yourself. You ought to know and show that you're someone special, that you're valuable, a person of quality. Therefore, you aren't for sale or for hire. You're not cheap; you're precious. And you expect to be treated that way.

That means you don't take the initiative. You don't chase after men; they chase you! You don't call them; they call you! You're God's *"good thing"* (Proverbs 18:22) that a man finds when he finds you!

That's not conceit; it's self-respect. If you don't respect yourself, then neither will anyone else.

Remember, know who you are in Christ.

You Hold the Key

And whatsoever ye do in word or deed, do all in the name of the Lord Jesus, giving thanks to God and the Father by him. (Colossians 3:17)

As a lady, you hold the key. By your attitude and actions, you will often decide whether your relationship with a young man is moral or immoral.

Let me explain what I mean. It's no secret that in the young man the sex urge is very strong, perhaps the driving force in his life at the moment. In fact, science tells us that the male sex drive reaches its height at about age 17 or 18 and then gradually decreases over the years. The female sex urge, however, is different. It doesn't reach its peak until the late twenties or early thirties. Even then it may never reach the proportions of the male urge. Therefore, it is only natural that the young man will be much more interested in and insistent upon fulfillment of that sex urge than will the female. That's just the way it is. These are the facts of life, so to speak.

As a young woman, you should know these so-called facts. Like it or not, in your relationships with young men, you will have to deal with these facts. Sometimes that may not be easy, especially when your own emotions become involved. That's why it's so important that you always remember who you are, your quality and worth in the eyes of God. If you are wise at all, you will want to maintain that worth. To do so, you will have to refuse to be treated as anything other than a lady.

You remember the story of Joseph, the man of God who was serving in the house of Potiphar, an official in Egypt. Time and again Potiphar's wife tried to seduce Joseph, but he always managed to avoid her advances—until one day when they were alone in the house and Potiphar's wife grabbed Joseph by the sleeve and tried to drag him bodily to bed with her. Do you remember Joseph's reaction? He slipped out of his coat and ran from the house, leaving his garment behind him in his haste. He left his coat, but he held on to his purity and righteousness. (See Genesis 39:7–13.)

Sad to say, there are all too few Josephs out there today. Because of the normal sex urge in a young man and the permissiveness of our society, he is not usually inclined to turn down such an opportunity. In fact, unless he is particularly strong spiritually, he will actively look for such opportunities! Generally speaking, because of their biological makeup, young men find it much harder to resist sexual temptation than young women do. That's why I say that, as a young woman, you hold the key to the morality of your relationship.

You should never feel obligated to repay a young man for taking you out by providing him with sexual favors. Don't ever let Satan trick you into thinking you owe any man your affection or the use of your body. That's one of the oldest lies in the world: "You owe me for all I've done for you!" Don't fall for that one! If a young man tries to use that line on you, that should tell you his estimation of you—and himself! You are not obligated to any man—except One, Jesus Christ. If a man doesn't think enough of you to respect your purity, he isn't worthy of you. And it wouldn't hurt to tell him so!

But besides sexual favors, there is the simple matter of exchanging "harmless" kisses and hugs. You should never feel obligated even to give a date a good-night kiss. In fact, there's no such thing as harmless kisses and hugs. Everybody affects you—whether the effect is good or bad. Why not believe God for a relationship free of physical touch (caressing, kissing, and so on) until marriage? Why amplify and magnify the appetites of the flesh unnecessarily? Why not follow after righteousness and flee youthful lusts? The Spirit of God wants to help you to discipline the flesh and remain pure until the honeymoon.

Remember, the test is Colossians 3:17: *"And whatsoever ye do in word or deed, do all in the name of the Lord Jesus, giving thanks to God and the Father by him."* Can you honestly say that what you are doing is being done in the name of Jesus, or that it is bringing glory to God? If not, then don't do it!

There is nothing wrong with kissing or hugging in the right context. The right context, as never before, is the marriage relationship. Remember, every stick of dynamite has a fuse. Hugging and kissing is the fuse that could cause your life to literally explode. AIDS, pregnancy, guilt, shame, depression, lust, and so on are sticks of dynamite waiting to be ignited by wrong decisions on your part. Remain a prized possession for God and your future mate. The Bible tells us not to *"give place to the devil"* (Ephesians 4:27), and *"whatever you do, whether in word or deed, do it all in the name of the Lord Jesus"* (Colossians 3:17 NIV). If you wouldn't do it in the very presence of the Lord Himself, then don't do it! Let that be your guide.

Remember, you hold the key.

may be, you have a certain amount of money on hand each week to spend. Start out by learning to budget. Remember, a budget is not just a record of spending; it is a *plan* for spending.

Sit down and plan your spending for a week or a month in advance. Then try to stay within your plan as closely as possible. As you learn to plan your spending, you will learn to remain within your income. That will be good training for you as your income begins to increase, especially once you are married, when you and your spouse can pool your resources.

Since the man is usually the principal bread-winner in the family, he must take the lead in financial planning. But both husband and wife can contribute to the overall financial well-being of the family. Let's look at several verses in Proverbs 31 that reveal practical ways a woman can contribute to the financial workings of her home.

Verse nineteen tells us that the virtuous woman (the good homemaker) *"layeth her hands to the spindle, and her hands hold the distaff."* This simply means she has learned how to sew. The good homemaker learns early how to take care of the material needs of her household.

Verse fifteen says that she *"giveth meat to her household."* This, of course, means that she knows

4

Your Body Belongs
to God

4

Your Body Belongs to God

The Temple of the Holy Spirit

*What? know ye not that your body is the temple
of the Holy Ghost which is in you, which ye have of
God, and ye are not your own? For ye are bought
with a price: therefore glorify God in your body,
and in your spirit, which are God's.*
—1 Corinthians 6:19–20

There is one good reason why you as a young woman should not allow any man to possess your body: Your body is not yours. It belongs to God. It is His holy temple.

When you became a Christian, the Holy Spirit came to take up residence in you. Your physical body became His temple. Therefore, despite what you may hear or even think or say, that body is no longer yours; it belongs to God.

That's why you must keep yourself pure. You are responsible for your body. You are God's temple guard!

You and I were created to have fellowship with God. We were created to commune with our Creator, to live for our Maker, to be in subjection to His Word.

When we live apart from Him, we are living an incomplete life, a life that is leading to destruction. The Bible declares that *"there is a way that seemeth right unto a man, but the end thereof are the ways of death"* (Proverbs 16:25). God did not create us for death, but for life. That life is found only in the Author of Life. The Author is also the Owner. Our bodies belong to God.

If that is true, then what should be your attitude toward anyone who would try to defile God's temple, your body? Suppose some young man tries to put pressure on you to have sex with him. Suppose he tells you that there's nothing wrong with it, that everybody's doing it, that if you truly love him you'll give in to his desires. What do you say then?

You say what God says. God says that fornication is a sin, and your body belongs to Him (1 Corinthians 6:18). Sexual union outside of marriage is wrong. It's immoral. It is a defilement of God's holy temple.

56

That's what you say to the young man and to yourself. You remind yourself that you are not your own, that you were bought with a price (verse 20). You tell that young man that if he really loved you, he would not insist, or even ask, that you go against your convictions. If he truly cared about you and not just the use of your body, then he would treat you with honor and dignity. He would respect your position as a child of God. If he doesn't do that, then he isn't worthy of you.

When a man tells you he loves you so much he just has to have you, he's really saying just the opposite. What he really means is that he wants you so much he'll say anything to get you! What he is really after is not you—it's just your body. He doesn't really care anything about you. If he did, he would show his love by the way he treats you. To him you're just a means of gratifying his lust—nothing more. And that's not true love; it's *self-love*.

When a man truly loves you, he won't want to do anything to harm you. He won't take chances with your body. He would never risk your being harmed by an unwanted pregnancy. He will be concerned for your good name, your personal convictions, your reputation in society, and your respect for yourself. He will think first of what's best for you, not what's satisfying to him. That's true love.

You may be going with a young man who is trying to get you involved in premarital sex. If so, you need to sever that relationship right now! Unless your partner values you enough to put your well-being ahead of his fleshly desires, then he's not worthy of you! If you continue that relationship, sooner or later you will be hurt, because it's not based on mutual love. It's one-sided. And one-sided love affairs never end well. Somebody always gets hurt. More than likely, it will be you.

Avoid Even the Appearance of Evil

"Abstain from all appearance of evil" (1 Thessalonians 5:22).

When I was dating Marilyn, there were times when I had to *"abstain from all appearance of evil."* I had to steer clear of certain situations that might have caused me to be led into temptation. If I hadn't, we might have become engaged in activities that would have been potentially harmful to both of us and our relationship together. I loved Marilyn so much, I didn't want to risk the possibility of losing her or causing her harm.

That's the way love works. It puts the welfare of the other person ahead of its own desires. Unless your young man is willing to do that for you, then he really doesn't love you. You need to face that fact—because it's true.

So in my case, I was a Joseph. I never had sex before marriage. I don't say that to boast; I give God all the glory for it. The reason I point it out is that so many people are saying that it can't be done, that young people today can't remain pure until marriage. That's just not so. Just as God helped me and Marilyn, He will also help you. He is *"no respecter of persons"* (Acts 10:34). What He did for us, He will do for anyone who puts his or her trust in Him. The Bible says that *"Jesus Christ* [is] *the same yesterday, and to day, and for ever"* (Hebrews 13:8). If you turn to Him for help, He'll keep you just as He kept us.

That's not to say that it was always easy for me to resist temptation. In my life and ministry I've had numerous chances to give in to temptation. Opportunity after opportunity has presented itself to me, but because of the power of the Holy Spirit and my commitment to God, I have always resisted. I have called upon the living God to deliver me from that temptation, and He has been faithful to do so. I am convinced He will continue to do so for me, and that He will do the same for you—if you really want Him to.

If you come under temptation and pressure, just turn your attention to the Word. Remind yourself that your body is not for fornication, but for the Lord (1 Corinthians 6:13). Remember that your body does not belong to you; it belongs to God. It's your duty and responsibility to keep it pure and holy.

Present Your Body to God

I beseech you therefore, brethren, by the mercies of God, that ye present your bodies a living sacrifice, holy, acceptable unto God, which is your reasonable service. (Romans 12:1)

When you are faced with temptation, you have a choice to make. You can decide to give your body to some man, or you can decide to present it unto your God. If I were you, I would choose to present it to God. It's to your benefit to do so.

Unless you do that, you cannot enjoy all the blessings that come from living in line with God's holy Word. As long as you are out of line with God's will for you as His child, you are living in conflict. Every desire, every drive you have will be frustrated until you come into harmony with your Maker, the One who designed your body. Once you yield to God and His will for you, then everything will begin to fall into place.

Nothing in this world can compare to a life lived in perfect harmony with our loving heavenly Father.

Yield to God, not Sin

Neither yield ye your members as instruments of unrighteousness unto sin: but yield yourselves unto God, as those that are alive from the dead, and your members as instruments of righteousness unto God. (Romans 6:13)

Again we see that we are not to yield to temptation and sin, but we are to yield to God and the power of His Holy Spirit within us. When you find yourself in a situation in which you are tempted to yield to fleshly desire, there will always be an accompanying desire to refuse that temptation. That desire is the voice of the Holy Spirit within you. Yield to His voice, not to the voice of your flesh.

Later on in Romans 6, Paul told us, *"Yield your members servants to righteousness unto holiness"* (verse 19). You and I have been redeemed from the curse of the law. We have been translated from the kingdom of darkness into the kingdom of God's own dear Son. While we were serving the Devil, all our members were his servants for iniquity and sin. Now that we are born again, now that we are in Christ Jesus, we have a new Master. No longer are we under obligation to Satan and sin; now we are subjects of the Most High God. Now we are to present our members (our bodies) in service to Him.

Once we were slaves of sin; now we have been set free to be servants of holiness and righteousness. We have been bought with a price—the precious blood of God's own Son. Therefore, we are not our own; we belong to God. That's why you are not free to give your body to any man. You already belong to Someone. It is your duty and responsibility to remain faithful to Him—until He provides for you the one man of His choice with whom you will become one flesh through the bonds of holy matrimony. If your young man is not willing to wait until then, then he is just that—your young man—and he's not God's man for you!

Remember, sexual union outside of marriage is not just a sin; it is treason against your Lord!

Flee Fornication

Meats for the belly, and the belly for meats: but God shall destroy both it and them. Now the body is not for fornication, but for the Lord; and the Lord for the body. And God hath both raised up the Lord, and will also raise up us by his own power. Know ye not that your bodies are the members of Christ? shall I then take the members of Christ, and make them the members of an harlot? God forbid. What? know ye not that he which is joined to an harlot is one body? for two, saith he, shall be one flesh. But he that is joined unto the Lord is one spirit. Flee fornication. Every sin that a man doeth is without the body; but he that committeth fornication sinneth against his own body.

(1 Corinthians 6:13–18)

Some young people ask me what difference it makes whether they are married or not when they engage in sex together. They say they don't see what difference a piece of paper (a marriage license) makes. They point out that since they intend to be married someday, they can't see where sexual union before then is wrong for them. Can you see where it is wrong?

Fornication is defined as sex outside of marriage. According to this passage, fornication is a sin. It is taking what is joined unto the Lord by the Spirit and joining it to another by the flesh. Can you see why God is not pleased with that kind of union?

The Word of God is quite explicit about this matter. The Lord says, *"Flee fornication"* (verse 18). That ought to be clear enough.

But why does God say to *"flee fornication"*? The answer is given in that same verse: *"Every sin that a man* [a person] *doeth is without the body; but he* [or she] *that committeth fornication sinneth against his* [or her] *own body."* Every time a person commits fornication, he or she stirs up an appetite that God never intended to be satisfied outside of marriage.

In Hebrews 13:4 we read, *"Marriage is honourable in all, and the bed undefiled: but whoremongers and adulterers God will judge."* One of the reasons God created and instituted marriage was to provide a means of fulfilling the wholesome sex urge. But this verse makes it clear that an attempt to fulfill that desire outside of marriage is condemned by God. One reason is that it cannot ever be totally fulfilled; it will always reoccur. Once a person engages in sex, that does not end his or her desire; it only serves to intensify it.

Paul spoke of people whose god is their belly—their lust or their sensual cravings (Philippians 3:19). The sexual appetite is like the physical appetite; it is not easily satisfied. Even when it is, it doesn't stay satisfied. Just as each new indulgence in overeating only serves to whet the appetite for more and richer foods, so it is with fleshly desires. Any attempt to satisfy them only causes them to increase in intensity and power. The end result is often total destruction of the person.

Uncontrolled sexual appetites lead to uncontrolled sexual activity. And that leads to all kinds of misery: venereal disease, unwanted pregnancies, abortions—to say nothing of guilt, shame, remorse, and shattered relationships. The best way to lose your young man is to give in to his sexual appetites and yours!

I once met a young lady who confessed to me that she had no control at all over her sexual conduct. She revealed that she had started engaging in sexual activity early in her life. Every time she had sex, her appetite was intensified. Finally, she had reached the point where she just couldn't help herself. She would give herself to almost any man anytime. As a result, she was miserable. She hated herself for what she was, yet she couldn't stop herself. The force she had unleashed within was stronger than she was. She was desperate for deliverance. That is precisely what is needed in such cases—deliverance.

Remember, uncontrolled passion leads to uncontrolled possession!

In my life and ministry I have met many young people who are slaves to their sexual passions. They have so intensified those lusts within, they have no more power to control them. Their minds have become twisted and sick. All they think of and talk about night and day is sex. They read pornographic magazines and books and watch "skin flicks" on television. They frequent cheap adult bookstores and theaters. They are constantly seeking sexual gratification. The result is not only shameful and disgusting; it is tragic.

Such people need help, not condemnation. But the sad thing is, many of them don't really *want* help. They are so far gone, they are seemingly beyond help, beyond hope. That's why God warns us to flee fornication. He knows what those sensual appetites can produce once they are stirred up. He also knows the final results of sexual sin, and they are not good.

I thank God for my mother. She always taught me, "Son, run from a woman who chases you. If you're not careful, she'll get you in trouble!" That's what God is telling us in these verses: "My child, run from fornication. If you're not careful, it'll get you in trouble!" And God knows what He's talking about!

One reason there is so much divorce today is an overindulgence in sexual activity before marriage. Today, couples who have been married for twenty-five and thirty years are suddenly getting a divorce. Why? Many times the only reason they have stayed together as long as they have is fear of public opinion. They were just afraid of what people might say if they split up. Now, with our lax standards, divorce is so common that nobody even raises an eyebrow. So all those people who have never been happy in their marriages are finally free to end them. And they do. Thousands of them every year.

Why is that? Why do so many marriages end in divorce? Many times it is because of unfulfilled sexual desires (*lusts* would be a better word). Many people who engaged in sex before marriage have a difficult time adjusting to just one sex partner. It isn't long before the thrill has gone out of their relationship. So either they end up having an affair outside the marriage or else they just settle down to boredom and unhappiness—until they get caught in that affair or until they can't stand the boredom any longer. Then comes the divorce.

This is just another reason why God warns us so strongly about stirring up the sexual appetite before marriage. It has effects not only before marriage, but also afterward. If you want a happy, stable marriage, don't play around before the wedding! If your boyfriend (or girlfriend) is not content to wait until after the ceremony to consummate the marriage, then you'd do well to end that relationship before it's too late. If your future partner can't be faithful to God (and doesn't want you to be), then maybe you should ask yourself how faithful he or she is going to be to you!

Remember, a person who doesn't reverence God will not respect God's child. If that child is you, it would be better for you not to become involved with that person. You'd do better to flee.

That was King David's problem. He didn't flee when he should have. He didn't avoid even the appearance of evil. You remember how he fell into sin with Bathsheba. He was simply walking on the rooftop of his house one evening when he saw this beautiful lady taking a bath. Right here is where he made his tragic mistake. Instead of turning away, he looked! He gave in to the temptation to fulfill *"the lust of the eyes"* (1 John 2:16). Next he inquired about who that lovely creature was. He gave into the lust of the mind (his imagination). Finally, he gave into *"the lust of the flesh"* (verse 16). As a result, he was led into adultery and murder. His family and kingdom were eventually torn apart because of it. That's the kind of thing that happens when people are drawn into sexual relationships outside of marriage: they suffer in some manner.

God does not want to see His children experience hurt and tragedy. That's why He warns us to flee fornication. He knows it won't be easy; it takes discipline. But God is always ready to help us overcome temptation, if we will allow Him.

If you have already fallen into temptation and sexual sin, that doesn't mean it's too late for you. God always stands ready to forgive and restore. When you were born again, the blood of Jesus took care of *all* your sins. Although you have missed the mark, you haven't fallen from grace. Despite your failure, you are still God's child, and He loves you. No matter what you have done in the past, you are still an heir of God and a joint-heir with Jesus Christ. You can still walk free in your mind and stand tall on the inside. All you need to do to restore your fellowship with your Lord and Father is to confess your sin and repent of it. God has promised in His Word that He will forgive you of that sin and cleanse you of all unrighteousness (1 John 1:9).

Once you have done that, then put your sin behind you. Forget about it. Begin life anew and afresh. In God's eyes, it is as though nothing ever happened to mar your fellowship with Him. You are as clean and pure as if you had never sinned at all! Walk in that newness of life, that wholeness and purity.

Do yourself a favor: conform your life to the Word of God. Flee fornication. Abstain from even the appearance of evil. In the long run, you'll be glad you did!

5

No Unbelievers!

No Unbelievers!

Righteousness and Unrighteousness

*For he [God] hath made him [Christ] to be sin for us,
who knew no sin; that we might be made the
righteousness of God in him.*
—2 Corinthians 5:21

When you became a child of God, you were made *"the righteousness of God"* in Christ Jesus. Righteousness—the very righteousness of Christ—was imputed to you by God, just as it was to Abraham in the Old Testament when he exercised faith in God. (See Romans 4:3, 11.)

Whether you think you are righteous or not, whether you *feel* righteous or not, does not matter. God says you are righteous because of your faith in His Son, Jesus Christ. In the eyes of God, you are a righteous person. That's all that matters. Your righteousness is not a result of your actions; it is solely dependent upon your relationship to Jesus Christ.

If that is so, then anyone who is not in Christ is unrighteous—not because of his actions, but because of his lack of relationship with the Son of God. Regardless of how moral and upstanding he or she might be, an unbeliever is unrighteous.

No Fellowship between the Two

> Be ye not unequally yoked together with unbelievers: for what fellowship hath righteousness with unrighteousness? and what communion hath light with darkness? (2 Corinthians 6:14)

What fellowship is there between righteousness and unrighteousness? None. Have you ever known a believer who was excited about the things of God and had a close relationship with someone who was wrapped up in sin and immorality? No! Why not? Because the two are just not compatible. The interests and attitudes of one conflict with those of the other. They just don't go together.

That's what Paul was saying in this passage. Righteousness and unrighteousness shouldn't "go together" (date each other) because they just don't "go together" (fit each other). They don't go together because they don't think alike. They don't think alike because they have totally different natures.

The second part of this verse asks, *"And what communion hath light with darkness?"* Jesus told His disciples, *"Ye are the light of the world"* (Matthew 5:14). If you are born again, you are *"the light of the world."* The person who is lost is in darkness. What communion is there between light and darkness? None. Light and darkness cannot commune (become one) because they are direct opposites. You cannot become one with an unsaved person; it's just not possible.

But that's the negative side of the picture. Let's look at the positive side. What fellowship is there between righteousness and righteousness? Total fellowship. What communion does light have with light? Perfect communion. Light fellowships with light totally. Light becomes one with light perfectly. There can be no better fellowship or communion than that which exists between two objects or persons who are exactly the same.

Now let's look again at the negative side. Suppose you who are righteous, you who are light, become joined in marriage to an unbeliever, an unrighteous person, someone in darkness. What kind of fellowship will you have together? None. What hope of communion (oneness) will there be? None. That's why the Word of God says very plainly not to be unequally yoked together with unbelievers. Any yoke, or union, between a believer and an unbeliever is bound to be unequal!

Remember, as a Christian, you cannot be *equally* yoked with an unbeliever.

No Agreement between the Two

And what agreement hath the temple of God with idols? for ye are the temple of the living God; as God hath said, I will dwell in them, and walk in them; and I will be their God, and they shall be my people. (2 Corinthians 6:16)

Now in this verse, Paul was not speaking of an actual building when he said that we are *"the temple of God."* He meant that because the Holy Spirit lives in us, our bodies are God's earthly place of residence. Those who are not born again do not have the Spirit of God in them. They have the spirit of the world. What agreement can there be between the Holy Spirit of God and the spirit of this world? None. The two just do not agree.

As a Christian, your body is the temple of almighty God. Jesus said that in marriage the man and woman become one flesh. Therefore, if you marry an unbeliever, if you become one flesh with that person, you bring an idol into the temple of God!

That's why it is so important that you not become involved with an unbeliever. If you are even dating an unsaved person, you should break off that relationship immediately! It cannot lead to anything good; it can only cause harm.

What Is the Solution?

Wherefore come out from among them, and be ye separate, saith the Lord, and touch not the unclean thing; and I will receive you, and will be a Father unto you, and ye shall be my sons and daughters, saith the Lord Almighty.

(2 Corinthians 6:17–18)

Here we see God's solution to this problem of righteousness and unrighteousness, light and darkness. He says that we Christians are to come out from among the unbelievers. We are to separate ourselves from them. We are not even to *"touch"* them.

Jude told us, *"And others save with fear, pulling them out of the fire; hating even the garment spotted by the flesh"* (Jude 23).

This does not literally mean that we are not to even come in contact with unbelievers, or that we are to actually hate their clothes. It simply means that we are not to allow ourselves to become contaminated by them. We who are righteous are to keep ourselves pure and clean. We are not to become involved in close personal relationships with unbelievers, because, like it or not, their ways do rub off on us.

That's why God tells us to come out from among them and be separate. If we will do that, He has promised that He will receive us; we will be His sons and daughters, and He will be our God and Father.

Beware of the Stranger

"The mouth of strange women is a deep pit: he that is abhorred of the LORD shall fall therein" (Proverbs 22:14).

"For a whore is a deep ditch; and a strange woman is a narrow pit" (Proverbs 23:27).

Notice whose mouth it is that is described as a *"deep pit."* The mouth of *"strange women."* This refers to women who are not in the family of God.

Any person who is not born again of the Spirit of God has a *"strange"* mouth. It cannot speak the things of God, because it is out of the abundance of the heart that the mouth speaks (Matthew 12:34). The unbeliever's heart cannot be full of the things of God because it is not full of the Spirit of God. Therefore, the unsaved person cannot speak as God speaks. His or her mouth is *"strange"* to God and to us.

Notice also that the mouth of this "strange woman" is likened to *"a deep pit."* Proverbs 23:27 says that *"a strange woman is a narrow pit."* Once a person has fallen into a deep and narrow pit, it is hard to get out of that situation. Similarly, getting involved with an unbeliever is a dangerous game to play. If you're not careful, you'll fall into that deep and narrow pit from which you will find it very hard to free yourself.

This applies not only to dating, but also to business and social relationships. Before you get too personally involved in any kind of relationship with an unbeliever, make sure you are not being led into a pit. That other person may not have your standards of honesty and integrity. You may find yourself in a partnership (yoked together) with someone who can drag you into all kinds of trouble and grief.

In 1 Kings 11:1–3 we read about a famous man who allowed himself to become involved with *"strange women"*:

But king Solomon loved many strange women, together with the daughter of Pharaoh, women of the Moabites, Ammonites, Edomites, Zidonians, and Hittites; of the nations concerning which the LORD *said unto the children of Israel, Ye shall not go in to them, neither shall they come in unto you: for surely they will turn away your heart after their gods: Solomon clave unto these in love. And he had seven hundred wives, princesses, and three hundred concubines: and his wives turned away his heart.*

Solomon was said to be the wisest man in all Israel, perhaps the wisest man who ever lived besides Jesus Christ. Yet he ruined his own life and the lives of many other people in his kingdom because he became involved with *"strange women."* He had seven hundred foreign wives and three hundred concubines. They led him into idolatry and every other kind of sin. Just as the Lord had warned, these women turned Solomon's heart away from God. Despite his great wisdom and the warning of the Almighty, Solomon allowed himself to be led astray by *"strange women."* The result was that his kingdom was divided, and his people were scattered and taken into captivity.

Samson is another example of a great man of God who allowed himself to be led into destruction by a strange woman, Delilah. Both of these men were destroyed to some degree because they thought they could have relationships with unbelieving women and still reap the blessings of God. They discovered too late that it just won't work.

Nor will it work for you. If you want to enjoy the blessings of God, you must keep yourself from being contaminated by strange women—and strange men, too!

Remember, the mouth of a stranger is a deep and narrow pit; it will get you into trouble!

No Exceptions

"Let God be true, but every man a liar" (Romans 3:4).

Now some people will say, "Yes, that may be true. Getting involved with unbelievers is unwise—as a general rule. But my relationship is an exception."

That's exactly what Solomon and Samson thought. That's what *every* Christian thinks who becomes involved with an unbeliever.

In the Bible, God has clearly warned His children not to become unequally yoked with unbelievers. He said that for a reason. The reason is that such a union cannot produce good fruit. Such a marriage is not solid because it's built on an unequal foundation.

I can't tell you the number of times I've had to sit down with and counsel some woman who thought she had found an exception to the rule. In one such instance, the woman married the man even after I advised her against it. As it turned out, the marriage became a living hell. The husband, who had been so sweet and understanding before the wedding, suddenly began to resent his wife's church association and activities. It wasn't long before he refused to go with her anymore. From there, it got worse. Soon he was refusing to allow her to go. He kept on applying pressure on her until finally he had succeeded in totally alienating her from the church.

That's the kind of thing that God warns about when He says that we are not to become unequally yoked with unbelievers. The prophet Amos asked, *"Can two walk together, except they be agreed?"* (Amos 3:3). The answer is no.

Some people will say, "Oh, but I can win my spouse to the Lord!" I don't know how many times I've heard that statement made by eager young Christians in love. And how many times I have seen just the opposite! Instead of the Christian winning the non-Christian, more often than not it has been the other way around. I would estimate that nine times out of ten, that unbelieving mate will *not* be won to the Lord after marriage. More likely he or she will influence the believer to give up the church, or at least the believer's spiritual zeal will begin to diminish.

Don't make the tragic mistake of trying to reform your mate after marriage. Most of the time, it just won't work! There may be exceptions to this law, but there are no exceptions to the command: Don't be unequally yoked with unbelievers!

Remember, if you want a Christian marriage, marry a Christian!

Judge by the Fruit

Beware of false prophets, which come to you in sheep's clothing, but inwardly they are ravening wolves. Ye shall know them by their fruits.
(Matthew 7:15–16)

You may be surprised by this, but just because a person is a Christian does not mean that he or she is the right marriage partner for you—especially when that person has just recently accepted the Lord at your urging. Many times a person will become a Christian just to please his fiancée. Christianity may not be anything to him but a means to get what he wants—marriage.

If your fiancé is a new Christian, give him some time to prove his faith before the marriage. Let him show forth some fruits of his salvation. Jesus said that it is by their fruits that people should be judged.

I can remember several instances in which a woman waited only long enough for her fiancé to make a profession of faith before the two got married. That is usually a mistake. I have seen many of those marriages fall completely apart or become a living hell. That new Christian needs time to show that he truly loves God, that he did sincerely accept the Lord Jesus into his heart and life. It takes time to produce fruit. It may be hard to wait for that fruit to appear, but it's always worth the wait.

I have heard many young people say, "Oh, but I can't live without my sweetheart." Just remember, if he or she is not God's choice for you, you won't be able to live *with* that person!

Let God Marry You!

"What therefore God hath joined together, let not man put asunder" (Matthew 19:6).

Wait on the Lord. Give Him a chance to bring the right marriage partner to you. Let Him do the choosing of your mate and the planning of your marriage. When it is God who does the joining together, no man will ever be able to put it asunder!

When you are faced with a decision about whether or not to marry a certain person, let God decide for you. Jesus said that you cannot serve both God and man. You and I must decide whom we will serve.

The Lord has said in His Word that we believers are not to become united with unbelievers. That means that if you are romantically involved with an unsaved person, you need to break off that relationship—even if it breaks your heart to do so. God will heal your heart. Not only that, He'll give you the real desire of your heart. He'll provide the right mate for you, the one you've been looking and waiting for all your life.

If you insist on holding on to the wrong one, that's exactly what you'll get—the wrong one. You cannot be happy with the wrong marriage partner. To hold on to the wrong person when God wants to give you the right one is an act of spiritual rebellion. It is to say to the Lord, "God, I don't believe You. I know what's best for me; You don't." You ought to know by now that such an attitude is not pleasing to God.

It is faith that pleases God (Hebrews 11:6). Faith causes Him to reward you with the desires of your heart. You must decide right now whom you will serve, whom you will trust—yourself or God. The choice is yours.

Remember, God gives the best to those who let Him do the choosing!

Rest in the Lord

"Rest in the LORD, and wait patiently for him: fret not thyself" (Psalm 37:7).

Although God has promised to give us the desires of our heart if we will commit our way unto Him, He has not promised instant gratification. God does give the best to those who leave the choice to Him, but He doesn't always provide that choice overnight. Hebrews 6:12 speaks of those who through faith and patience inherit the promises of God. It takes not only faith to inherit the promises of God, but also *patience.*

You should make this commitment: "Lord, I will never marry an unbeliever. If need be, I will die single rather than marry the wrong person. I covenant to wait upon You to bring to me the one You have chosen as my life partner."

Once you have made your commitment to allow God to provide the one who is right for you, then you need to determine down in your spirit to rest in the Lord and wait patiently for Him. You must realize that even the Creator of the universe uses time to bring things to pass.

This is where patience comes in. It's wonderful to have great faith, but faith without patience never inherits the promises of God. You need to have such trust in God that you will remain single the rest of your life, if need be, rather than go against the will of God. When you come to the place where you are determined to have God's best for you even if you have to wait for it for eternity, then it may not be very long in coming!

This is because God sees the heart. Once He sees that you are firmly and totally committed to Him, once He is assured that you are determined that He is going to have the desires of His heart, then that's usually when He goes to work to see that you get the desires of your heart.

There have been a few people in my ministry who have made that kind of total commitment to God and His will. Today every one of them is happily married. And they are married to believers. Every one of them! When I ask some of them, "What ever happened to that person you once said you couldn't live without?" they usually answer, "What person?"

God honors His Word. When He promises to give you the desires of your heart, He means what He says. He watches over His Word to perform it (Jeremiah 1:12). He is looking for men and women who will take Him at His Word. When He finds such people, He takes great pleasure in performing His Word for them. But the way God recognizes such people is by watching them use their faith and patience. He watches to see if they hold fast to His Word of promise—come what may.

That's why the writer of Hebrews exhorted us, *"Let us hold fast the profession of our faith without wavering; (for he is faithful that promised)....Cast not away therefore your confidence, which hath great recompense of reward"* (Hebrews 10:23, 35). The *New International Version* translates this passage, *"Let us hold unswervingly to the hope we prossess, for he who promised is faithful....So do not throw away your confidence; it will be richly rewarded."*

Once you have committed your way to the Lord, rest in Him. Don't worry yourself with it any longer. Leave everything to your heavenly Father. You just take care of the Lord's business, and He will take care of yours. Just be about your Father's business. Don't chase after a man or a woman; let that person chase you. Don't seek a mate; seek out someone you can edify. Don't go out looking for popularity; instead, look for people to minister to. Your concern should not be "how to win friends and influence people," but how to win others to Christ. Concern yourself with seeing how you can be a blessing to others each day. As you do that, as you are busy about God's business, He'll be busy about yours. He'll be putting that right man or woman in a strategic place to cross your path at just the right moment.

Whether you know it or not, you have a divine appointment with destiny. Don't worry about how you are going to arrange everything just right so you will meet Mr. or Miss Right. Leave the details to God. You just follow Him, and He'll lead you right where you need to be at the very instant you need to be there!

When I left Detroit, Michigan, to attend Oral Roberts University in Tulsa, Oklahoma, I had no idea that I would meet a young lady from Nassau, Bahamas, who would become my "one and only." But the Lord knew! He worked out every detail, simply because we had each made the commitment to allow Him to bring us to the right person for us. We entrusted our lives to God, and He fulfilled that trust by providing us with the perfect match. But He did it in a way that neither of us would ever have imagined. That's God's way!

What the Lord did for Marilyn and me, He will do for you. If you will put your trust in Him and wait on Him in faith and patience, He will lead you to the one He has chosen for you.

Don't pray that the unbeliever you are now dating will get saved so that you two can get married. I've heard some young people say, "I'm just going to pray my boyfriend (or girlfriend) into the kingdom of God so that we can get married. Agree with me that this will happen." I won't do it.

Neither should you. That's selfish. And selfish prayers don't work. God says that we are not to get involved with unbelievers. It's fine to pray for an unsaved person's salvation, but not just so that you can get married to that person. That's not God's way. If you are that intimately involved with that person, you need to break off that relationship. If he or she is the one for you, the Lord will work it out. If not, you will be much better off without him or her.

And don't make the mistake of thinking that you can go out with an unbeliever and not get involved. Don't tell yourself, "Oh, I know I'll never marry this person, but it won't hurt to date him (or her)." Feelings and emotions are not that easy to control. Before you know it, you may become much more involved than you ever meant to be. You may find yourself compromising. You may start praying, "Oh, Lord, save my boyfriend (or girlfriend) so that we can be married! But if You don't, we're going to get married anyway because I can't live without him (or her)." That is setting the stage for trouble!

Remember, it's easier to *stay* out of trouble than to *get* out of trouble! And the best way to stay out of trouble is to trust the Lord and let Him work things out for the best.

Rest in the Lord. Wait patiently upon Him. If you will do that, He will give you the desires of your heart.

6

Some Practical Considerations

6

Some Practical
Considerations

Neither My Place nor Yours!

A good name is rather to be chosen than great riches.
—Proverbs 22:1

If you are a young person living away from
your parents, you should know that your apartment or residence is not the proper place to
entertain a date. Nor should you go to his or
her apartment. The Bible warns us to avoid even
the appearance of evil. No matter how casual or
innocent your relationship with a person of the
opposite sex might be, any unchaperoned private
meeting is dangerous—not only to your physical
and spiritual well-being, but also to your reputation, especially if you are a young woman.

In this age of sexual permissiveness and perversion, anything can happen—and does! Nowadays, no one is safe on the streets, much less in seclusion! Kidnapping, sexual assault, rape, murder—all these are everyday occurrences. Today you must be very careful with whom you associate, even publicly. You certainly don't need to put yourself in situations beyond your control. The results could be tragic.

Besides the physical harm that could result from being alone with someone you don't really know (or someone you only *think* you know well), there is the harm that can be done to your good name. In the Bible, we read that *"a good name is rather to be chosen than great riches."* Whether you realize it or not, people do see. And they do talk.

Many times when I teach this truth, young people will say, "So what? Let them talk. I don't care what people think or say."

That may be your reaction. But whether or not you care what people think and say, your heavenly Father cares. He is very much interested in what kind of reputation His children have in this world. That is because, like any parent, our Father is known through His children. As Christians, we bear the name of Jesus Christ. We need to be careful with His name—and our own. If you really don't care what people think, you at least ought to care what God thinks.

And God thinks we ought to have a good name and keep it!

The world judges our Father by us. If they see us involved in the same kind of questionable activities they are involved in, then they will naturally decide that there's nothing to this "church stuff." They will conclude that we Christians are nothing but hypocrites; we preach holiness but deep down we're no better than they are. Therefore, they decide they don't need what we have. If the unsaved see us Christians engaged in immorality, then they will condemn not only us, but also Christianity as a whole. Like it or not, we believers are responsible for the name we bear. God is not pleased when His children damage His good name!

Christians ought to have the best names in society. Creditors shouldn't have any problem with Christians. Believers should pay their bills. It's sad to say, but over the years some preachers have developed a bad name with creditors. Many times it's hard for a preacher to get credit because preachers, in general, have such a poor credit rating. It is an affront to God when His own spokesmen are known as financial risks. It is also an insult to God when His children are known as moral risks.

In Romans 13:14 Paul told us, *"But put ye on the Lord Jesus Christ, and make not provision for the flesh, to fulfil the lusts thereof."* What Paul was saying here is, "Don't get yourself into situations where you might be tempted to give in to carnal desire." If you invite your date to your apartment, or agree to go to his or hers, you are making *"provision for the flesh."* You are consciously exposing yourself to temptation. You may tell yourself that you can handle it, and maybe you can. But your date may not be able to handle it. You may end up doing something you hadn't intended to do.

The Bible says to *"make not provision for the flesh,"* but to *"put…on the Lord Jesus Christ."* Jesus Christ would not knowingly put Himself into temptation. So the point is not whether you can handle temptation or not; it's whether you are wise and obedient enough to avoid it. If you will do that, you will preserve your good name.

As a Christian young person, you may not be able to do anything about the bad name some preachers have with lenders and creditors. But there is something you can do about your own name in society. You can keep it good. One way to do that is to avoid even the appearance of evil. That means that your answer to the popular question, "My place or yours?" must always be, "Neither!"

Remember, a good name is worth more than great riches! Don't throw away your treasure!

The Word Is Integrity!

"The integrity of the upright shall guide them" (Proverbs 11:3).

When the Bible speaks of integrity, it refers primarily to honesty. As a Christian, you should be honest in your relationships with others. That means you should not lead someone on. People who do that have an ulterior motive. They just want to take advantage of others.

As a child of God, you must not be guilty of that kind of selfishness and dishonesty. If someone shows an interest in you and you do not really care for them, then politely say so. Don't pretend or put on a false front. It's better to be open and straightforward about your feelings than it is to lead someone into thinking you care for him or her when you really don't.

It may be good for your ego to keep someone on the string. It may make you feel important to have several people running after you. But it's not good for them. It's not fair to keep someone else dangling when you have no intention of returning that affection. In the long run, it's kinder to lay your cards on the table right from the beginning than it is to string someone along. Put yourself in that person's shoes. Treat him or her as you would want to be treated if the situation were reversed. God is not pleased when His children toy with people's affections.

By the same token, when you find yourself getting serious about someone, be honest about it. Keep your feelings out in the open. Let the other party know how you feel. If he or she is right for you, your honesty will work for you. If that person is not right for you, it's better to find out before you get too deeply involved. Otherwise, you may wind up with a broken heart.

Before you find yourself getting serious about someone, take time to find out whether he or she is a Christian or not. If you're not bold enough to come right out and ask, then just be observant. Watch how that person acts. Note how he or she treats other people, especially his or her parents! There is an old saying: "If you want to know how a man will treat you after you're married, watch how he treats his mother." That applies equally well to a young woman. If you want to know what kind of a wife she'll be, observe what kind of a daughter she is.

It doesn't take a great gift of discernment to be able to tell whether someone is a believer and whether or not he is actively serving the Lord. Just listen to his speech for a while. Notice how he dresses, where he wants to go on dates, what activities he enjoys. See how much Word there is in his walk as well as in his talk! It won't be long before his true nature and character will come out. When it does, you will know whether he is really a Christian or not. If not, then you need to end that relationship as quickly as possible.

Never make the mistake of thinking you can reform another person. If he hasn't changed in the many years *before* he met you, it's not very likely he will change *after* meeting you.

Remember, when God provides you with His choice, you won't have to do an overhaul on that person! If you have to change someone to make him or her right for you, then that person is wrong for you. It's just that simple!

Finally, never use spiritual matters as an excuse to avoid going out with someone you don't really care for. I have heard some young ladies say that they couldn't go out on a date because they needed to stay home and spend more time in the Word. That's ridiculous. It's dishonest. Never use God as a scapegoat. If you're not interested in going out with a person, then say so. You can do it tactfully but honestly. Just say, "Thank you for asking, but I really don't want to go out with you." Although no fellow likes to hear that from a young lady, he would rather be told the truth than to be fed a line.

The *New International Version* of Proverbs 24:26 says, *"An honest answer is like a kiss on the lips.*" Although no one likes to be hurt, everyone appreciates the truth. Honesty is the best policy in these situations, because in the long run the kindest thing you can do for a person is to tell him or her the truth.

Remember, the rule is this: Be firm but walk in love. But the best way to walk in love with someone is to be honest with him. Preserve your integrity. It will always be your best guide.

A Godly Appearance

"Deck thyself now with majesty and excellency; and array thyself with glory and beauty" (Job 40:10).

Beauty is God's idea and invention. Solomon told us that God *"hath made every thing beautiful in his time"* (Ecclesiastes 3:11).

Not only did God conceive and invent beauty, but He Himself is beautiful. Beauty is one of His attributes. The psalmist wrote, *"One thing have I desired of the LORD, that will I seek after; that I may dwell in the house of the LORD all the days of my life, to behold the beauty of the LORD"* (Psalm 27:4).

Besides being beautiful Himself, God's offspring are beautiful. Isaiah told us, *"In that day shall the branch of the LORD be beautiful and glorious"* (Isaiah 4:2).

If God and all His creation are beautiful, then it seems reasonable that He desires for His children to be beautiful also. In the verse from Job 40, God declares to His servant that if he is to be like his Lord, he must deck himself with majesty and excellence, and array himself with glory and beauty.

What does this mean to us as believers today? It simply means that we are to do our utmost to look our best at all times—especially when we go out in public. That is not only good advice, but also practical counsel, particularly for the young and unmarried. As a single young adult, you never know when you're going to meet for the first time that very special person in your life! Therefore, the wisest thing for you to do is to dress and groom yourself just as though this is the moment of that historic meeting!

That means, young lady, that if you haven't been wearing makeup, you need to learn how.

But you say, "Oh, but I want to be holy!"

Then be beautiful! First Chronicles says, *"Worship the* LORD *in the **beauty** of holiness"* (1 Chronicles 16:29, emphasis added). One way to be holy is to be beautiful.

Then you may say, "But I thought the Bible taught that women were not to depend upon outward adornment, but to have beautiful inner spirits."

That's true. Godly women are to be beautiful on the inside. But if God desires interior beauty, then it stands to reason that He also desires outward beauty. Holiness doesn't mean wearing long shapeless dresses, no makeup, and your hair tied up in a bun. Holiness is an attitude of the heart. Sanctification means being set apart unto God. You are holy by what you have in your heart, not by what you put on your back. That doesn't mean we are to dress immodestly like some unbelievers. It simply means that we are not to be bound by tradition. Wearing a long black dress down to the ankles and closed-in shoes doesn't make a person any bit holier than wearing a stylish three-piece suit and Bally shoes!

Our outward appearance is to be a reflection of our inward state. When Christ comes into a person's heart, He brings joy, peace, freedom, abundance, beauty. That's what should be reflected on the outside. That's why a Christian's manner of dress should be modest but fashionable, stylish but neither drab nor outlandish. In other words, the Christian's outward appearance should be as attractive and appealing as His Lord.

You and I are God's children. We ought to look the part. When we go to buy a car, are we satisfied with one that just has a beautiful interior? Don't we want the exterior to be as lovely as the interior? Of course we do.

If you have a preference, wouldn't you rather be seen with an attractive date than with one who is sloppy and unkempt? Does anyone really want to go out with a slob? Don't you yourself want to be thought of as good-looking? Where do you think that desire for a pleasing outward appearance comes from? It's part of the nature of God that is in us. Every born-again child of God has within him or her a desire for beauty of face and form. That is part of the nature of a Christian, having an appreciation of true beauty. We have that nature within us because we have the Spirit of God inside us. Our God is a God of beauty.

All through the Bible we read about the beauty of God's creation, the heavens and the earth. In heaven there are gates of pearl and streets of gold. There is a river as clear as crystal. There is a multicolored rainbow around God's throne. The members of His royal court are dressed in splendid white robes, so bright that they defy description.

If you study the Old Testament, you will see that the Jewish tabernacle and temple were built according to God's specifications. They were magnificently beautiful—decorated with gold and silver and polished brass; adorned with rich, vibrant colors; resplendent with light. The dress of the priests and Levites was also carefully designed by God to impress the worshippers with its richness and beauty.

Make no mistake about it, our God likes for things to be beautiful! That includes His children—you and me. That means that whenever we go out, we ought to look our very best. We ought to dress neatly and conservatively. We ought to be clean and well-groomed. Our shoes should be shined, our hair neatly combed, our clothes freshly pressed, our teeth brushed, our breath clean, and our faces lit up with a smile!

Sure, that takes a little extra effort! A good outward appearance requires preparation. That's why I'm writing about these things. I want to make sure you understand what being a child of God is all about.

Can you imagine Prince Charles of Great Britain going out in public looking like you and I do sometimes? Royalty can't afford to be lax in their appearance. They know that every time they stick their heads out the door of the palace, they are going to be examined, scrutinized, photographed. Not only do they have to always be on their best behavior, but they also have to be seen in their best outfits. That's part of their job as nobility, as members of the British royal family.

Well, I have news for you—you and I are also nobility! We are members of the royal family of the King of Kings and the Lord of Lords! We need not only to act the part, but also to learn to look the part!

Remember, you are a child of the God of beauty! Learn to act and look like what you are!

Conclusion

Make the quality decision to serve Jesus with all your heart, mind, body, soul, and strength. The apostle Peter told us to cast all our care on God, because He cares for us (1 Peter 5:7). If you will only cast *all* of your cares, worries, and problems upon the Lord, He will work them out. Remember, you are precious to your heavenly Father.

In 1 Timothy 4:12, Paul wrote to his young disciple in the faith, *"Be thou an example of the believers, in word, in conversation, in charity, in spirit, in faith, in purity."* Like Timothy, you, too, are an example to the body of Christ. But more than that, God is depending on you to be an example to the unbelievers, as well. If you will determine in your heart to be a good example for your brothers and sisters in Christ, you will automatically be a model for the unsaved.

If you feel that you have failed the Lord by your words or actions in the past, then receive

God's forgiveness and restore your fellowship
with Him by praying this prayer:

> Heavenly Father, in the name of Jesus I face
> up to the sin in my life that has affected our
> fellowship together. I confess that sin to You. I
> repent of it now as an act of my will. I ask You
> to forgive me of that sin and to cleanse me from
> all unrighteousness in accordance with 1 John
> 1:9. I receive my forgiveness now, and I thank
> You for it in Jesus' name.
>
> I thank You, Father, for Your love and mercy,
> and I yield myself to You as a vessel of righteous-
> ness unto holiness.
>
> In Jesus' name. Amen.

If you have never received Jesus as your personal Savior and Lord, and you sense the desire
and need to do that, pray this prayer out loud:

> Dear God, I am a sinner. I need Jesus. I
> believe in my heart and confess with my mouth
> that You raised Him from the dead.
>
> Jesus, I ask You to come into my life. I con-
> fess You as my Savior and my Lord.
>
> Dear God, thank You for saving me and for
> accepting me into Your family. I now call You
> my very own Father.
>
> In Jesus' name. Amen.

About the Author

Robyn Gool was born February 11, 1953, in Detroit, Michigan. At age nine he received Jesus as his Savior and also began traveling around the country playing tennis. In pursuit of a sports career, he accepted a tennis scholarship from Oral Roberts University. While at ORU, Robyn received the gift of the Holy Spirit and was called into Christian ministry in December 1972.

It was also at ORU that Pastor Gool met Marilyn, the young lady from Nassau, Bahamas, who was later to become his wife. From this union came three beautiful children: Robyn Johms, Marilyn Joi, and Sanchia Jentle.

In 1980 God led Robyn and Marilyn to begin an independent work in Charlotte, North Carolina. That work, Victory Christian Center, has grown in many ways since July 1980. At present, Sunday morning attendance runs over 2,000, and a full volunteer staff supports nursery, children's, and adult Bible classes. The outreach ministry, More than Conquerors Ministries, includes a daily television and radio program aired locally, a Bible school for laymen, and a school of ministry for those called into the ministry.

Pastor Gool has appeared on the Inspirational Network, Lester Sumrall's LESEA *Alive* telecast, and *Richard Roberts Live*. He has shared the Word of God both nationally and internationally for various ministries.

Other Books by
Robyn Gool

Don't Block the Blessings

Proper Attitudes toward Leadership

From Pressure to Praise

What to Do When You're Backed against the Wall

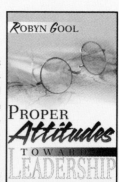